Count on CGP in the KS1 Maths SATs!

This CGP book is packed with SATs-style Maths questions split up into stress-free 10-Minute Tests. It's a brilliant way to help pupils prepare for the real SATs.

There's plenty of practice for both the Arithmetic and Reasoning papers, and all the answers are included in a cut-out-and-keep section!

What CGP is all about

Our sole aim here at CGP is to produce the highest quality books — carefully written, immaculately presented and dangerously close to being funny.

Then we work our socks off to get them out to you — at the cheapest possible prices.

Contents

Set A

Test 1 2
Test 2 6
Test 3 10
Test 4 14
Arithmetic Test 18
Scoresheet 21

Set B

Test 1 22
Test 2 26
Test 3 30
Test 4 34
Arithmetic Test 38
Scoresheet 41

Set C

Test 1	42
Test 2	46
Test 3	50
Test 4	54
Arithmetic Test	58
Scoresheet	61
Answers	62
Progress Chart	71

Just like in the real tests, calculators are not allowed.

Published by CGP

Editors: Izzy Bowen, Emma Cleasby and Ruth Wilbourne
With thanks to Alan Jones and Karen Wells for the proofreading.
Also thanks to Laura Jakubowski for the copyright research.

Coin images on pages 4, 9, 21, 23, 44, 52, 62, 63, 65 and 68 © iStock.com

ISBN: 978 1 78294 708 0
Clipart from Corel®
Printed by Elanders Ltd, Newcastle upon Tyne.
Based on the classic CGP style created by Richard Parsons.

Text, design, layout and original illustrations © Coordination Group Publications Ltd. (CGP) 2017
All rights reserved.

**Photocopying this book is not permitted, even if you have a CLA licence.
Extra copies are available from CGP with next day delivery • 0800 1712 712 • www.cgpbooks.co.uk**

Set A: Test 1

There are **9 questions**. Give yourself **10 minutes** to answer them.

1. Join pairs of words to make these four numbers.
   One has been done for you.

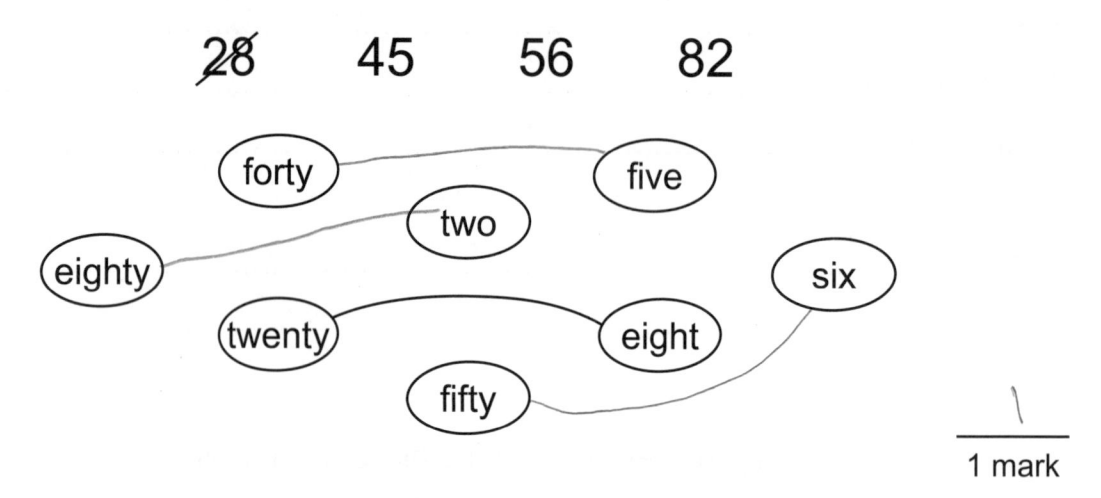

   ~~28~~   45   56   82

   forty — five
   eighty — two
   twenty — eight
   fifty — six

   1 mark

2. Circle **all** of the shapes with **5 sides**.

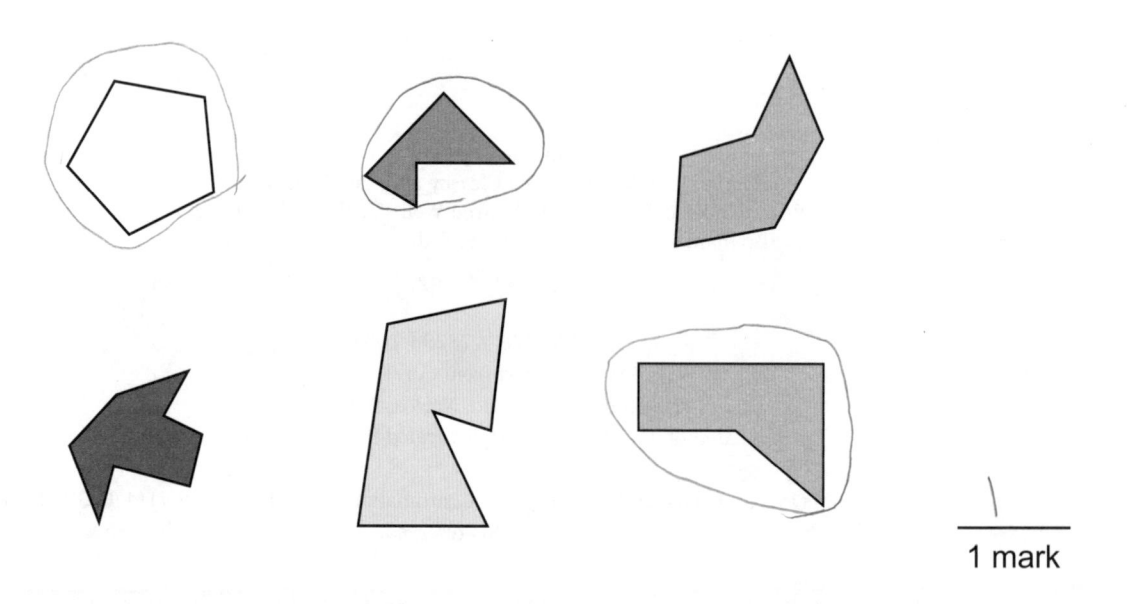

   1 mark

Set A: Test 1   2   © CGP — not to be photocopied

3. Use these units to complete the sentences.

ml   cm   kg

A tiger weighs 100 [Kg].

A mouse is 8 [cm] long.

There is 300 [ml] of juice in my bottle.

1 mark

4. This table shows the pets at the vet's.

Pet	Number of pets
Cats	6
Dogs	8
Rabbits	2

How many pets were at the vet's **in total**?

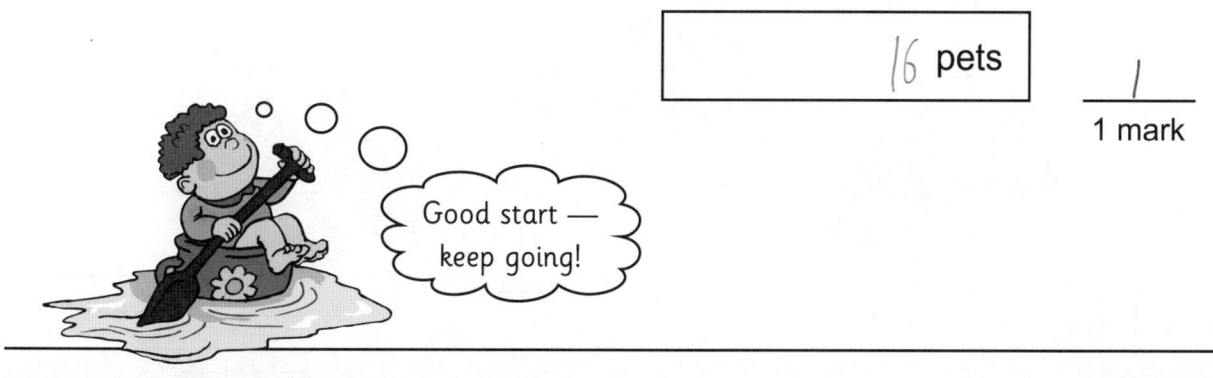

[16] pets

1 mark

Good start — keep going!

© CGP — not to be photocopied   3   Set A: Test 1

5. Tick the number sentence that is correct.

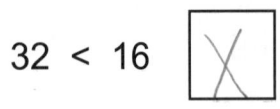

    32 < 16 ☒   52 > 45 ☑

    83 > 90 ☒   17 + 0 > 17 ☒

    1 mark

6. A pie is cut into **6** slices.

    Misha gives Tim $\frac{1}{3}$ of the pie.

    How many slices does she give Tim?

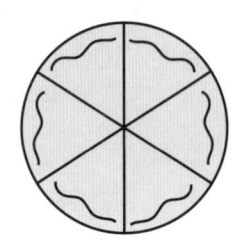

    2 slices

    1 mark

7. Safa has these coins.

    Circle the group of coins that makes the **same amount**.

    1 mark

Set A: Test 1

8. The arrow is rotated by a **three-quarter** turn **clockwise**.

   Draw the arrow **after** it has been rotated.

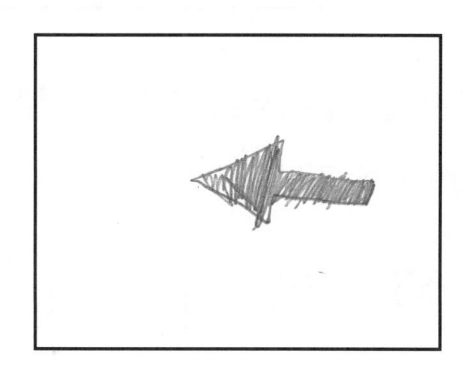

   [arrow drawn pointing left]

   ✓
   1 mark

9. There are **36** people on a bus.

   17 people get off the bus.

   At the next stop **11** more people get off the bus.

   How many people are on the bus now?

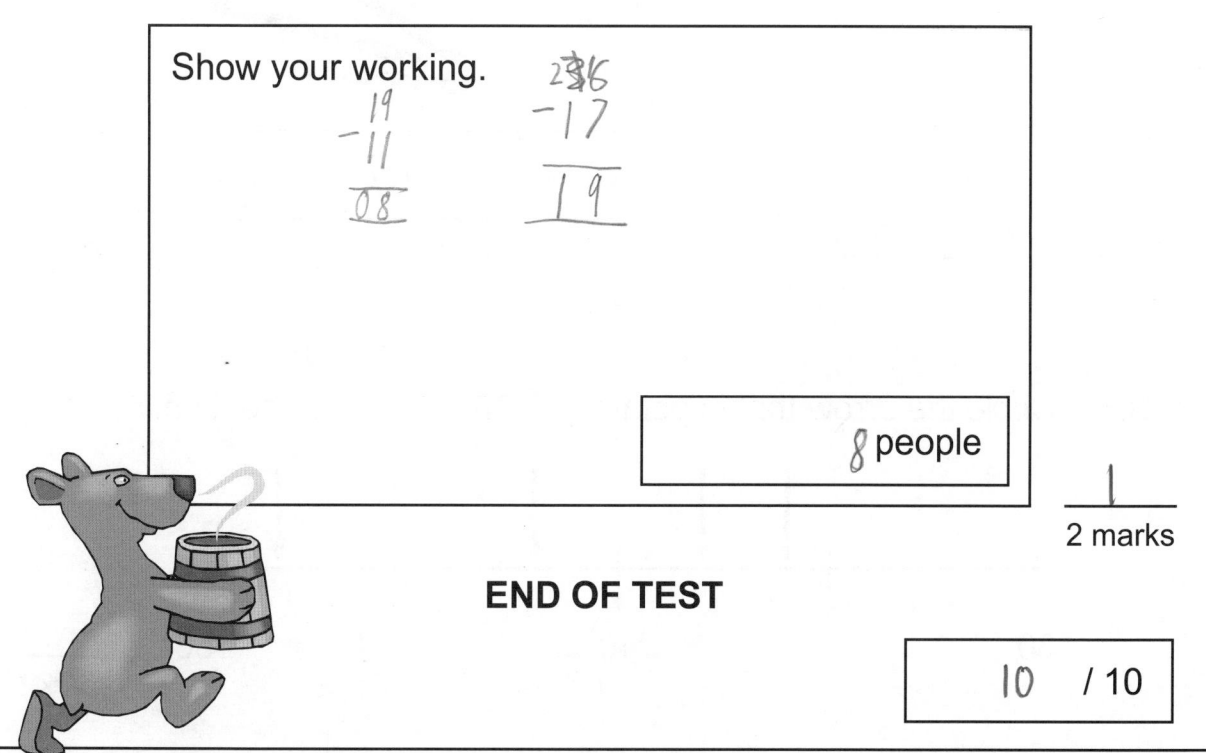

   Show your working.

   19   2̶3̶6̶
   -11   -17
   ───   ───
   08   19

   8 people

   ✓
   2 marks

END OF TEST

10 / 10

Set A: Test 2

There are **9 questions**. Give yourself **10 minutes** to answer them.

1. Bindu makes this sequence of **odd numbers**.

   Fill in the missing numbers.

   51   53   55 | 57 | 59 | ~~41~~ 61 |

   1 mark

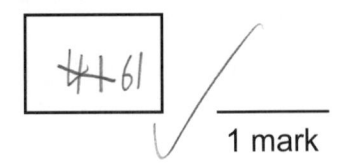

2. Dale has **29** pencils.

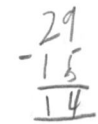

   15 of the pencils are red. The rest are green.

   How many **green** pencils does he have?

   $$\begin{array}{r} 29 \\ -15 \\ \hline 14 \end{array}$$

   | 14 green pencils |

   1 mark

3. Circle the arrow that is pointing to **38** on the number line.

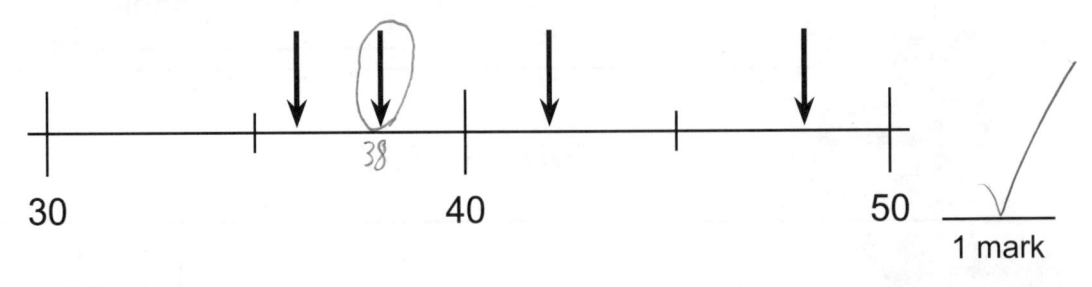

   (second arrow circled, labelled 38)

   30   40   50

   1 mark

Set A: Test 2

4. How much does the broccoli weigh?

250 grams

✓

1 mark

5. The clocks show when some children set off for school.

Dan   Jess   Jack

Who set off **first**?

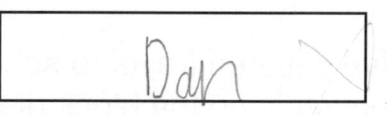

Dan

1 mark

6. There are **24** books in a classroom.

   Mr Khan gives out **half** of the books.

   How many books does he give out?

   ☐ 12 books

   1 mark

7. This block diagram shows how the children in Mr Woods' class travel to school.

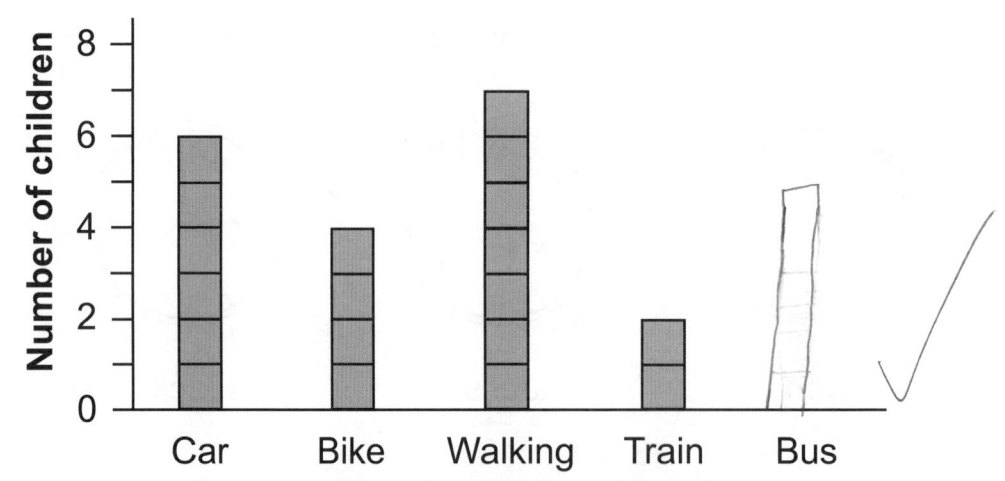

   Five children travel to school on the **bus**.
   Show this on the block diagram.

   How many **more** children **walk** than get the **train**?

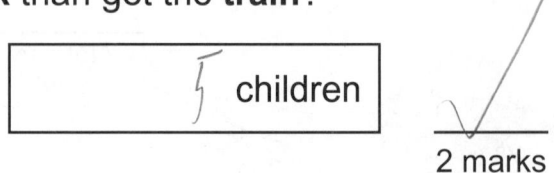

   ☐ 5 children

   2 marks

8. A supermarket has **9** tills.

   There are **5** people waiting at each till.

   How many people are waiting **in total**?

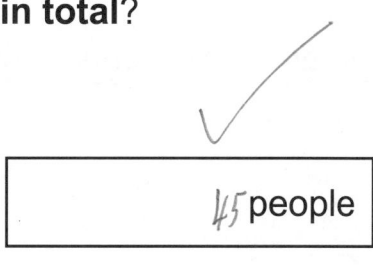

   ☐ 45 people ✓

   1 mark

9. Nancy buys a bracelet for **85p**.

   She gives the shopkeeper **3** coins and gets **5p change**.

   Circle the coins she uses.

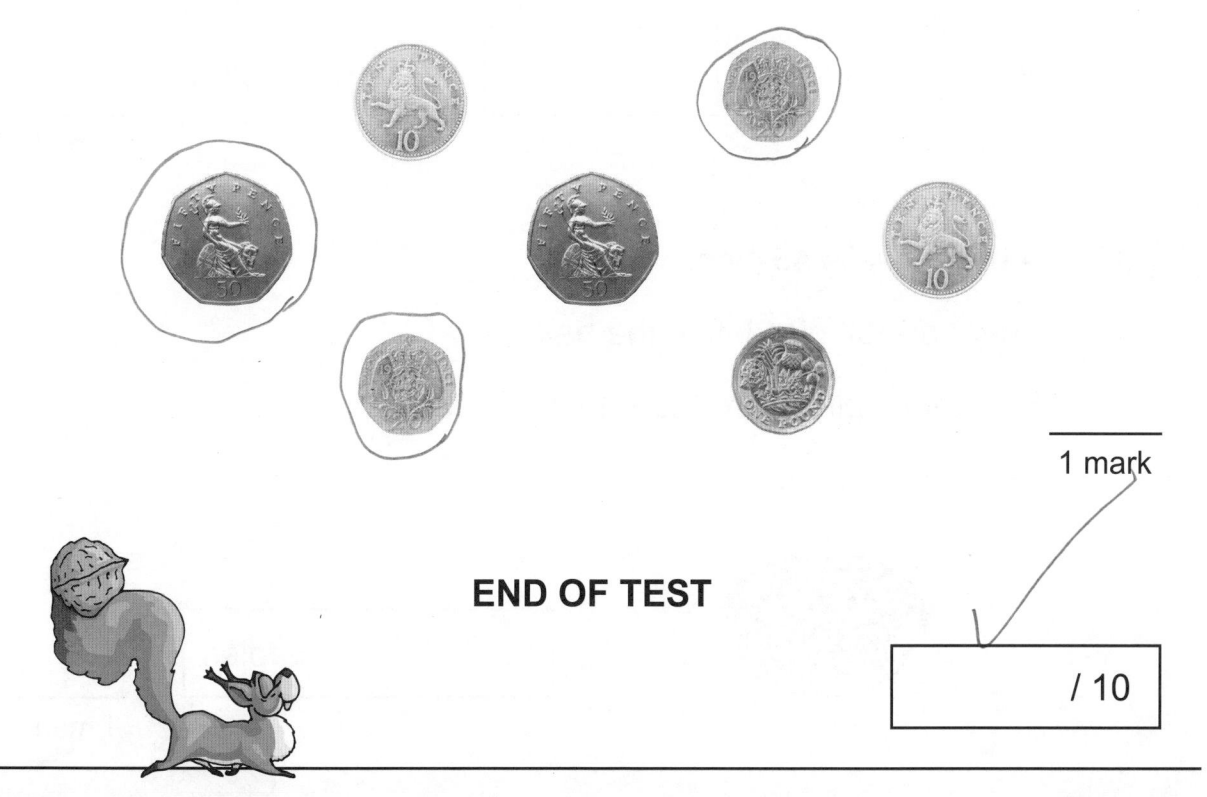

   1 mark

END OF TEST

/ 10

Set A: Test 3

There are **9 questions**. Give yourself **10 minutes** to answer them.

1. Circle **all** of the numbers that have **more than 3 tens**.

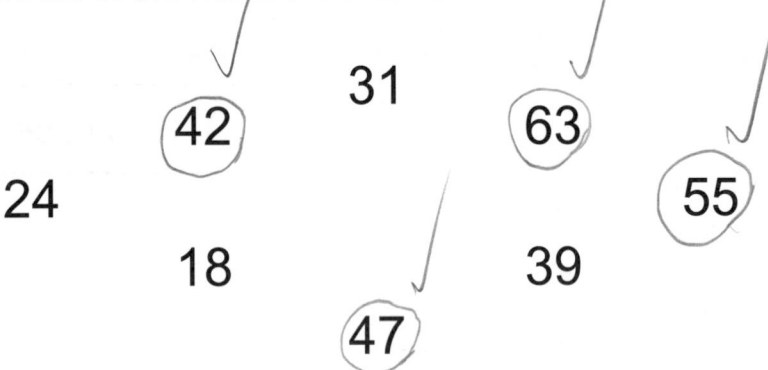

    24   (42)   31   (63)   (55)
          18   39
          (47)

    _____
    1 mark

2. Look at this sequence of months.
   Fill in the missing month.

   March   April | May | June   July

    _____
    1 mark

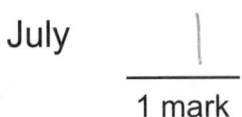

3. A bakery sells **45** pies.

   There are **32** pies left in the bakery.

   How many pies were there to begin with?

   | 77 | pies

    _____
    1 mark

4. This pictogram shows how many apples some horses ate today.

| | ◯ stands for → 1 apple |

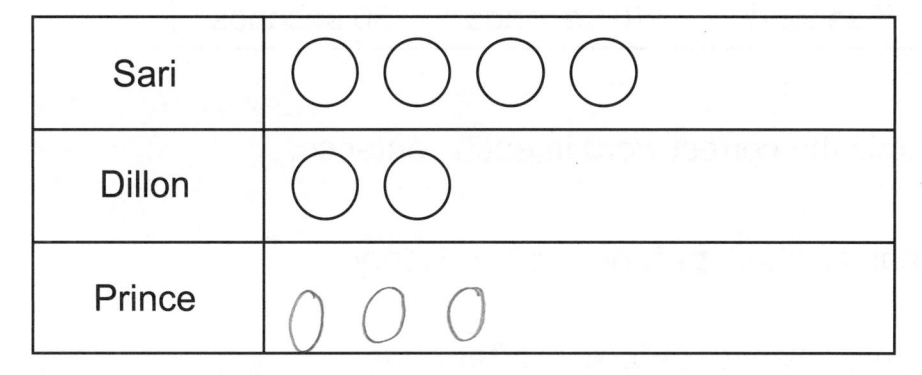

Sari	◯ ◯ ◯ ◯
Dillon	◯ ◯
Prince	◯ ◯ ◯

Prince ate **three** apples today.
Add this to the pictogram.

1 mark

5. Tick the shape that has the **most square faces**.

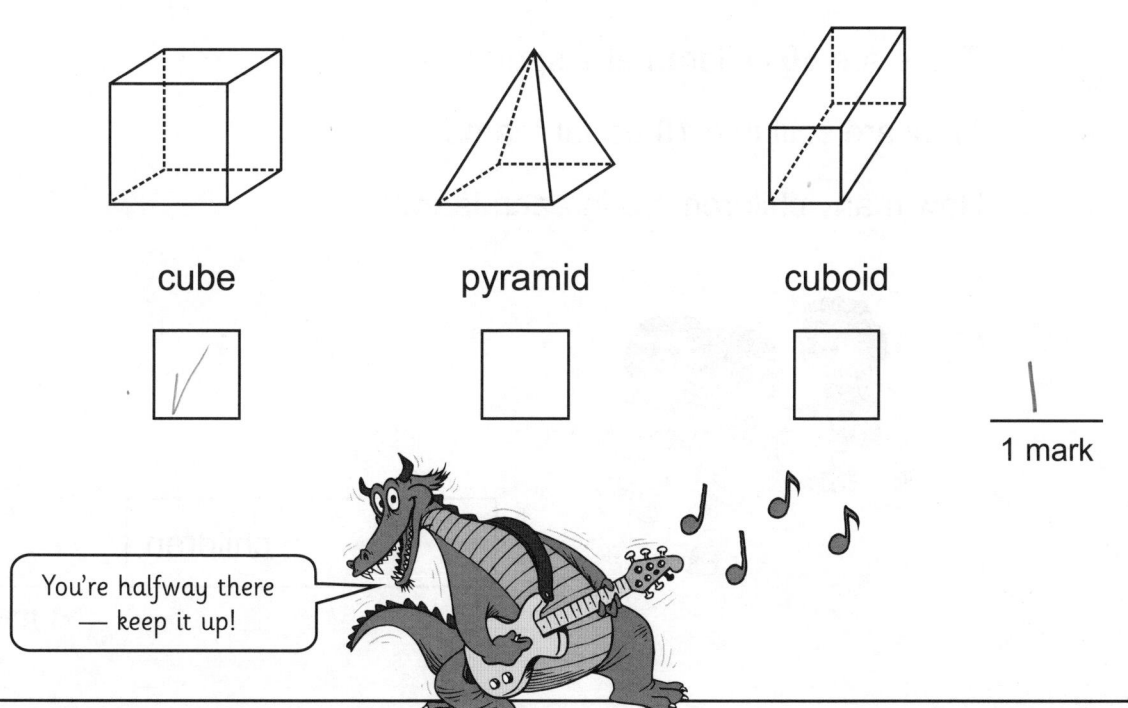

cube pyramid cuboid

[✓] [ ] [ ]

1 mark

You're halfway there — keep it up!

6. Three children had a race. Their times are written below.

Tina	Henry	Leah
4 minutes 5 seconds	5 minutes 10 seconds	4 minutes 50 seconds

Circle the correct word in each sentence.

Leah finished **(before)** / after Henry.

Henry finished before / **(after)** Tina.

Tina was the **(first)** / last to finish.

1 mark: 1

7. There are **80** children at a sports day.

They are split into **10** equal teams.

How many children are in each team?

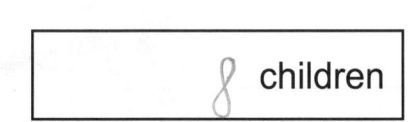

$80 \div 10 = 8$

8 children

1 mark: 1

8. What **fraction** of each shape is coloured in?

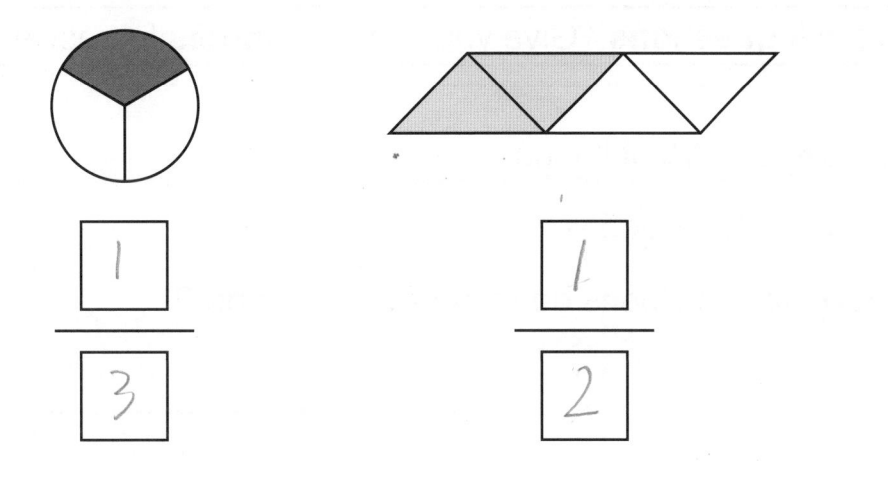

$\frac{1}{3}$ 　　　　 $\frac{1}{2}$

2 marks

9. Adil spends **90p** in a shop.

He buys a ruler for **30p**.

Circle the other **two** items that he buys.

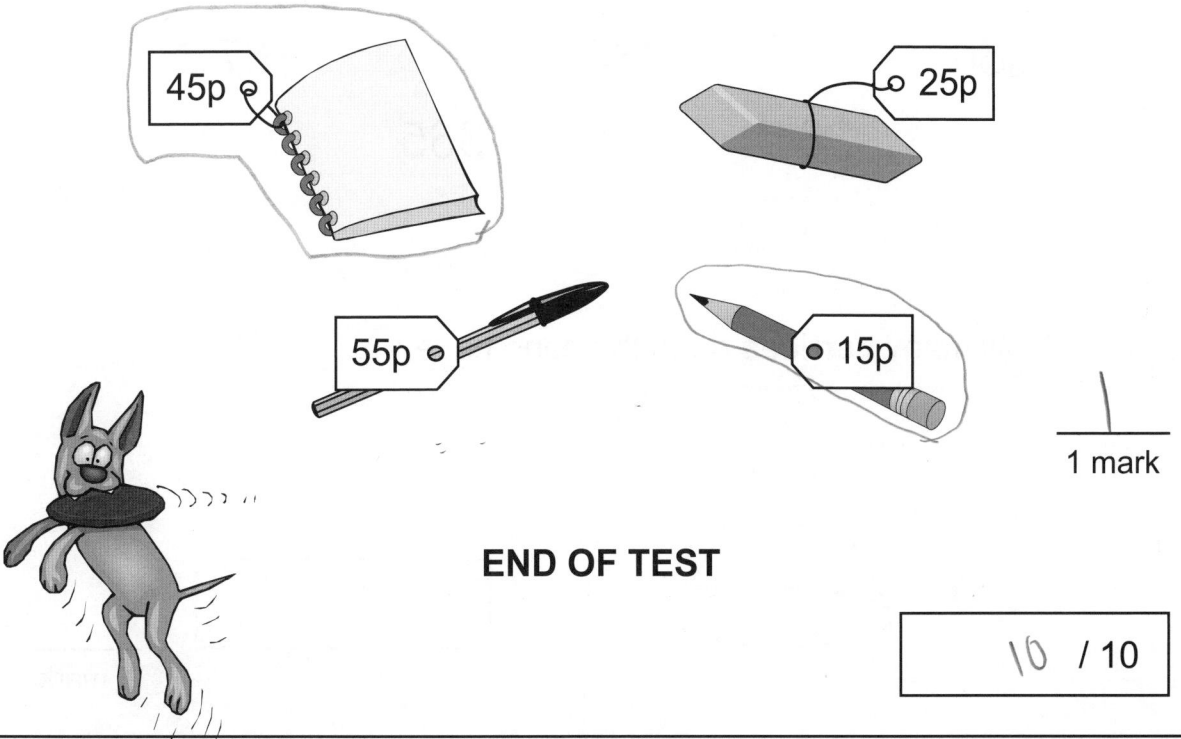

45p　　25p

55p　　15p

1 mark

END OF TEST

10 / 10

Set A: Test 4

There are **9 questions**. Give yourself **10 minutes** to answer them.

1. Wesley has **19** balloons.

   Milly has **20** balloons.

   How many balloons do they have altogether?

   39 balloons

   1 mark

2. A leap year is **one day longer** than a normal year.
   Circle the number of days in a **leap year**.

   360   (366)   367
       (364)   365

   1 mark

3. How many **vertices** does the cone have? 1

   1 mark

4. Circle the **two** numbers that are in the **wrong** places in this sequence.

22   32   42   (82)   62   72   (52)

1 mark

5. This tally chart shows the favourite sports of the children in Tanya's class.

Sport	Tally
Football	|||| |||| ||||
Swimming	|||| ||||
Netball	|||| ||||

How many **more** children like **football** than netball?

5 children

1 mark

6. Here are the heights of some buildings.
Sort the buildings from **shortest** to **tallest**.

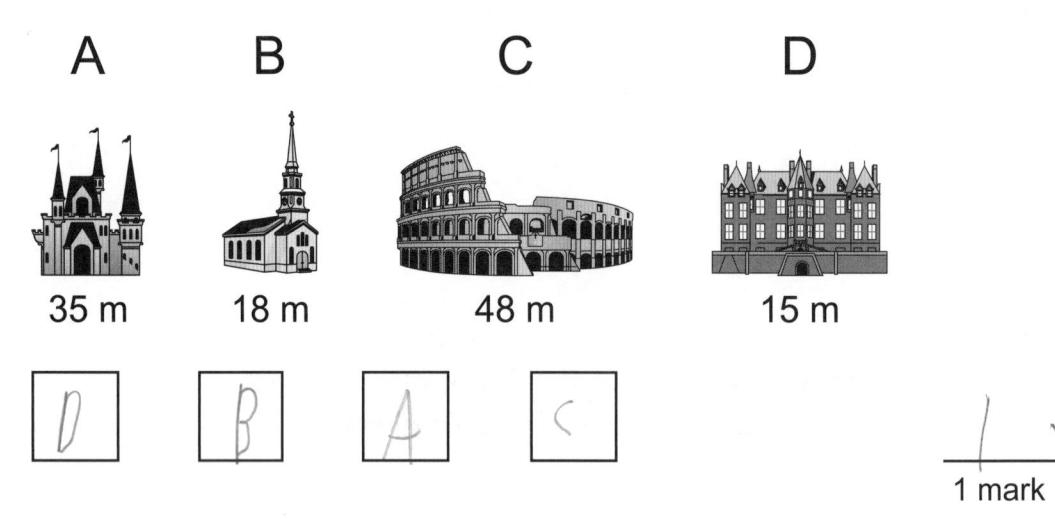

A — 35 m
B — 18 m
C — 48 m
D — 15 m

| D | B | A | C |

1 mark ✓

7. There are **9** presents in a bag.

Liam puts in **7** more presents.

Sally takes out **3** presents.

How many presents are in the bag now?

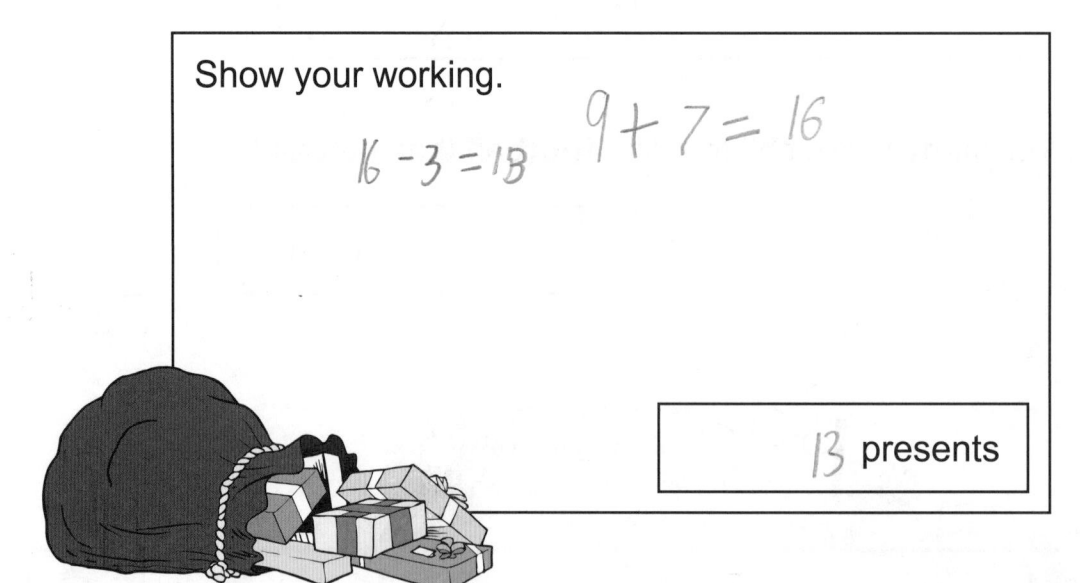

Show your working.

16 − 3 = 13   9 + 7 = 16

13 presents

2 marks ✓

8. Fill in the boxes so all **three** sums have the same answer.

$$22 + 64 = 86$$

$$42 + \boxed{44} = 86 \qquad \boxed{12} + 74$$

1 mark

9. There is a shape missing from this pattern.

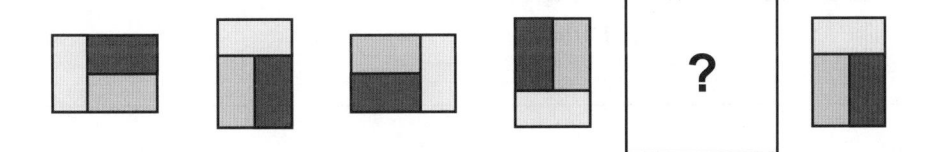

Draw a ring around the shape that goes in the box.

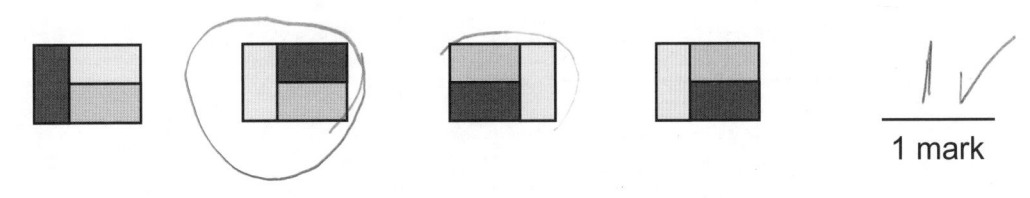

1 mark

END OF TEST

10 / 10

Set A: Arithmetic Test

There are **12 questions**. Give yourself **10 minutes** to answer them.

1. 8 + 4

   [12]

   1 mark

2. [30] + 3 = 33

   1 mark

3. 67 − 17

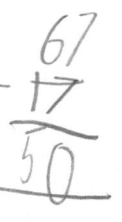

   $$\begin{array}{r} 67 \\ -17 \\ \hline 50 \end{array}$$

   [50]

   1 mark

4. 2 × 7

   [14]

   1 mark

5. 44 + 27

$$\begin{array}{r}44\\+27\\\hline 71\\1\end{array}$$

[71]   1 mark

6. 56 − 10 − 10

[36]   1 mark

7. 6 + 9 + 7

[22]   1 mark

8. 10 × 6

[60]   1 mark

9. $\frac{1}{2}$ of 22

11

1 mark

10. 77 − [57] = 20

1 mark

11. 45 ÷ 5

9

1 mark

12. $\frac{3}{4}$ of 40

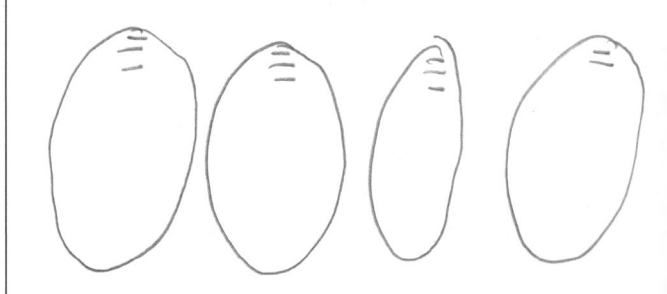

30

1 mark

END OF TEST / 12

Set A: Arithmetic Test

End of Set A: Scoresheet

You've finished a full set of tests — well done!

Put your scores in here
to see how you're doing...

	Score	
Test 1		/10
Test 2		/10
Test 3		/10
Test 4		/10
Arithmetic Test		/12
Total		**/52**

...then look up your total score to see what's next:

0 – 17	You might need some **more practice**. Ask an adult to help, then try the tests again.
18 – 35	**Go back** over the questions you got **wrong**, then try the **next set** of tests.
36 – 52	Well done! Try to beat your score on the **next set** of tests.

But first... bend your brain round this:

How many different ways can you make £1 using these coins?

This page may be photocopied

Set A: Scoresheet

Set B: Test 1

There are **9 questions**. Give yourself **10 minutes** to answer them.

1. Here are some digit cards.

   [5] [3] [7] [2]

   Circle **all** of the numbers that could be made by putting **two** of these cards together.

   thirty-six   **twenty-nine**   **fifty-four**

   (**seventy-three**)   (**twenty-five**)

   1 mark

2. Draw the next **four** shapes in this pattern.

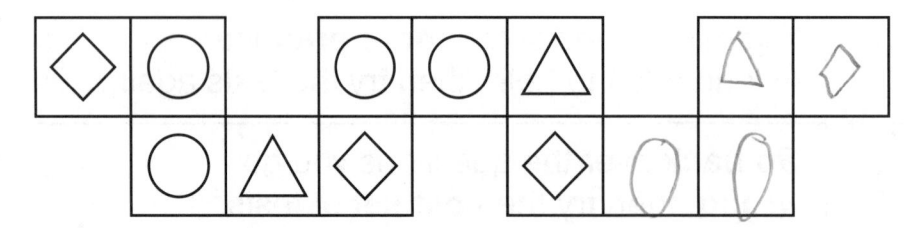

   1 mark

3. Tick the **two** sentences that are correct.

There are **6 days** in a week.	There are **24 hours** in a day.	There are **31 days** in June.	There are **12 months** in a year.
☐	✓	☐	✓

   1 mark

Set B: Test 1

4. Amir has these coins.

He buys a bouncy ball for **35p**.

Circle the **three** coins that he uses.

1 mark

5. Chelsea weighs two toys.

Write **>**, **<** or **=** in the gap to make the sentence correct.

weight of spinner [>] weight of car

1 mark

6. This block diagram shows the animals Lee saw in a park today.

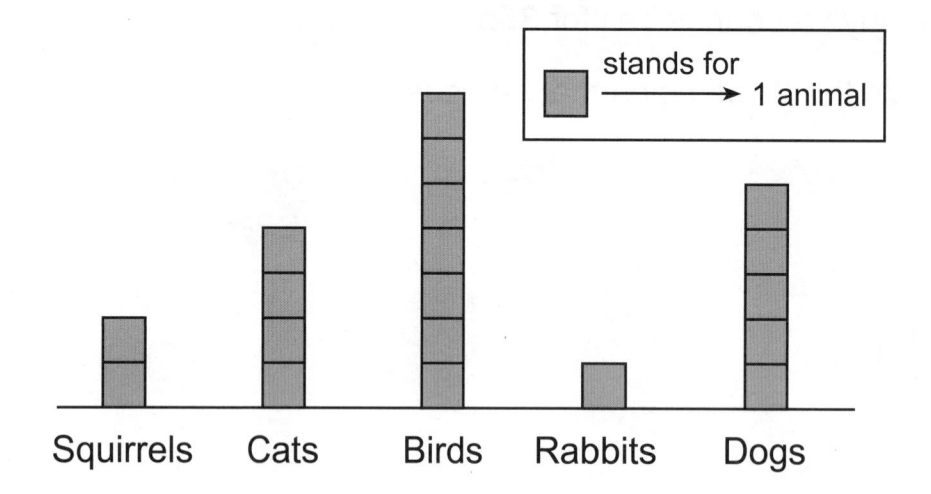

☐ stands for → 1 animal

Squirrels   Cats   Birds   Rabbits   Dogs

How many **more** birds than dogs did Lee see?

2 birds

1 mark

7. Tasha sells **half** of her sheep.

She has **10** sheep left.

How many sheep did Tasha have to begin with?

20 sheep

1 mark

8. **Estimate** the numbers that the arrows are pointing to.

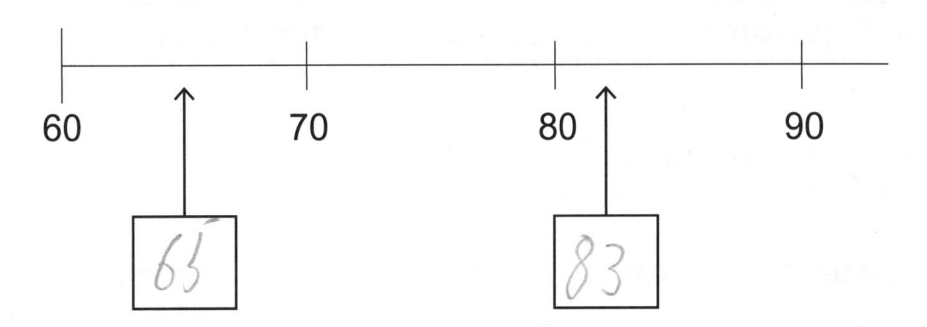

60   70   80   90

65   *83*

2 marks

9. Liz has **72** blackberries.

She uses **53** blackberries to make a pie.

How many blackberries are left?

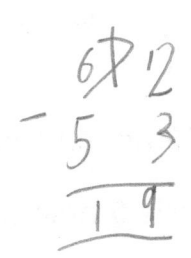

```
  6̶ 12
- 5  3
  1  9
```

19 blackberries

1 mark

END OF TEST

/ 10

Set B: Test 2

There are **9 questions**. Give yourself **10 minutes** to answer them.

1. Draw an arrow in each box to match the **direction** given for each object.

   backwards **up** **forwards** **down**

   1 mark

2. There are **32** animals in a pet shop.

   The shop sells **9** animals.

   How many animals does the shop have now?

   _____ animals

   1 mark

3. Draw a ring around **all** of the shapes that have **12 edges**.

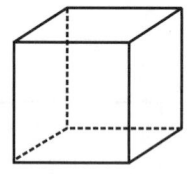

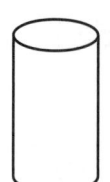

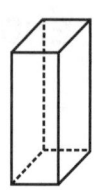

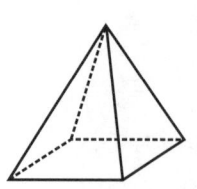

   1 mark

4. This table shows how long it took some cars to finish a race.

Car	Time
red car	25 seconds
green car	1 minute
blue car	45 seconds

Circle the correct word in each sentence.

The green car was **quicker** / **slower** than the red car.

The red car finished **before** / **after** the blue car.

1 mark

5. The first six numbers of a sequence have been shaded.

Shade the next **three** numbers in the sequence.

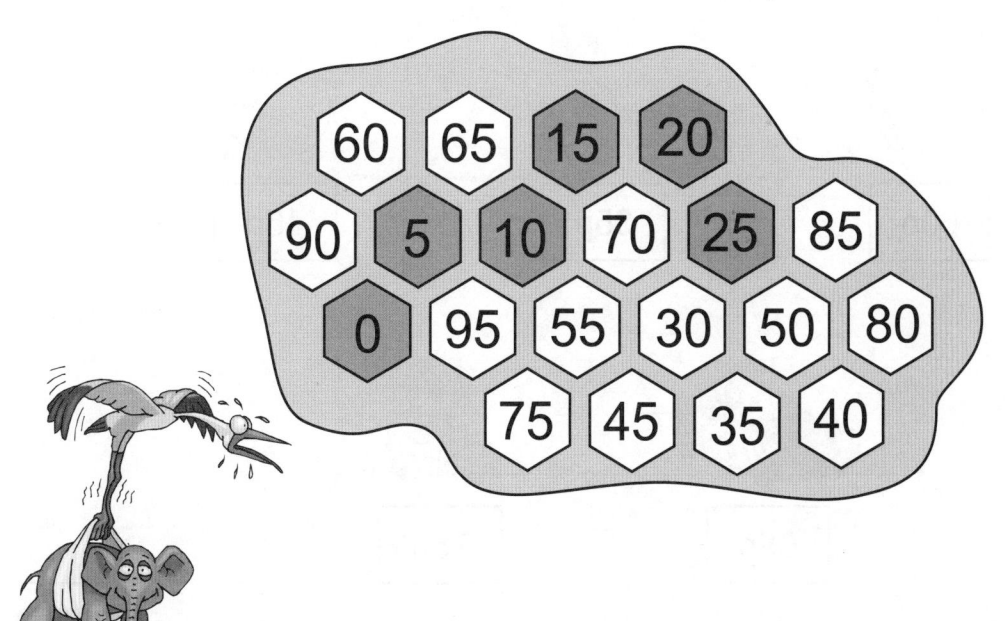

60 65 15 20
90 5 10 70 25 85
0 95 55 30 50 80
75 45 35 40

1 mark

6. This tally chart shows the favourite meals of Sam's class.

   Fill in the missing information.

Meal	Tally	Total
Pizza	丗 丗 I	
Roast Dinner		8
Curry	IIII	

   1 mark

7. Alice gives **80p** to a shopkeeper. She gets **15p change**. Circle the thing that she buys.

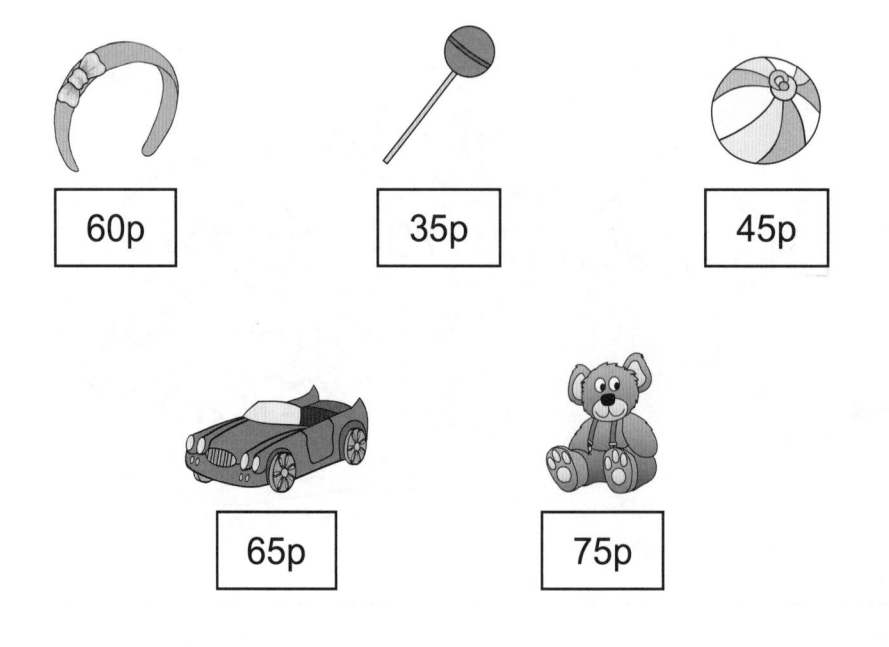

   60p   35p   45p

   65p   75p

   1 mark

Set B: Test 2

8. Look at this calculation.

$$47 - 10 = 37$$

Circle **two** calculations that you could use to check the answer.

10 − 47

37 + 10   37 − 10

47 + 10   47 − 37

_____
1 mark

9. There are **27** children in Yasmin's football club.

8 more boys and **9** more girls join the club.

How many children are in the club now?

Show your working.

children

_____
2 marks

END OF TEST

/ 10

Set B: Test 3

There are **9 questions**. Give yourself **10 minutes** to answer them.

1. Draw lines to match each description with the correct number.

   one **more** than fifty-three   55

   one **less** than sixty-five   53

   two **more** than fifty-one   64

   three **less** than fifty-eight   54

   1 mark

2. What shape is the grey face?

   Draw a ring around the name of the shape.

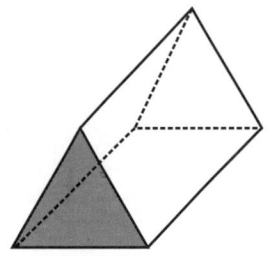

   Rectangle   **Square**

        Pentagon   **Triangle**

   1 mark

3. How many **minutes** are there in **1 hour**?

| minutes |

1 mark

4. What is the volume of the liquid in the tube?

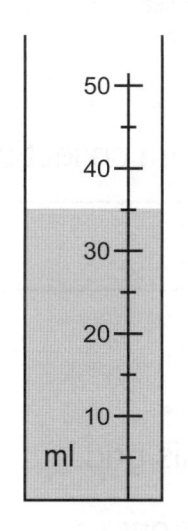

| ml |

1 mark

5. Cross out the boxes where the calculations inside do **not** have the same answer.

| 50 − 15 and 15 − 50 | | 50 + 15 and 15 + 50 |

| 2 × 6 and 6 × 2 | | 2 ÷ 6 and 6 ÷ 2 |

1 mark

Half way, keep going!

6. This chart shows how many leaves Rani and her friends collected at the park.

Rani	🍁 🍁
Harry	🍁 🍁 🍁
Sarah	🍁 🍁 🍁 🍁 🍁

🍁 stands for → 1 leaf

How many **fewer** leaves did **Rani** collect than **Sarah**?

[ ] leaves

1 mark

7. Dean stands in the centre of this grid.

He faces the direction of the arrow and follows these instructions.

1) Do **three** right angle turns **clockwise** and then jump forward **two** squares.

2) Do a **quarter** turn **anti-clockwise**.

3) Jump forward **three** squares and stop.

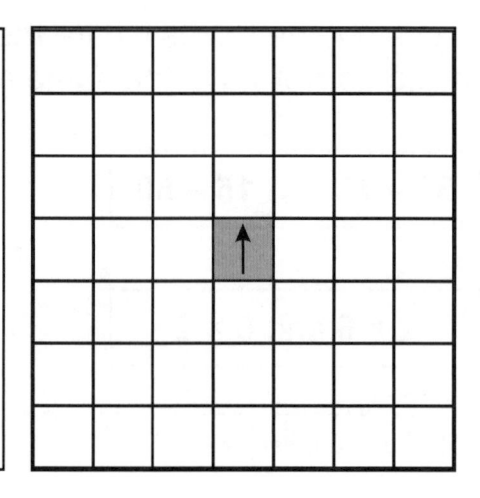

Draw a cross in the square where he stops.

1 mark

8. There are **6** tables in a classroom.

   There are **5** children sitting at each table.

   How many children are there altogether?

   | | children |

   1 mark

9. There are **83** coins in a treasure chest.

   Ryan takes **30** coins out of the chest.

   Mel puts **7** coins into the chest.

   How many coins are in the chest now?

   Show your working.

   | | coins |

   2 marks

   END OF TEST

   / 10

Set B: Test 4

There are **9 questions**. Give yourself **10 minutes** to answer them.

1. Cross out **all** the objects that are **not squares**.

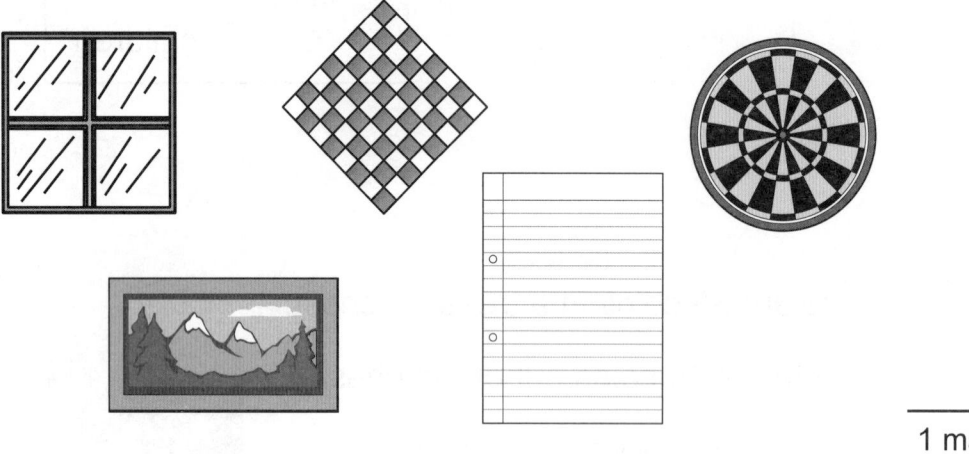

   1 mark

2. Put the numbers in the castle in order.
   Start with the **smallest**.

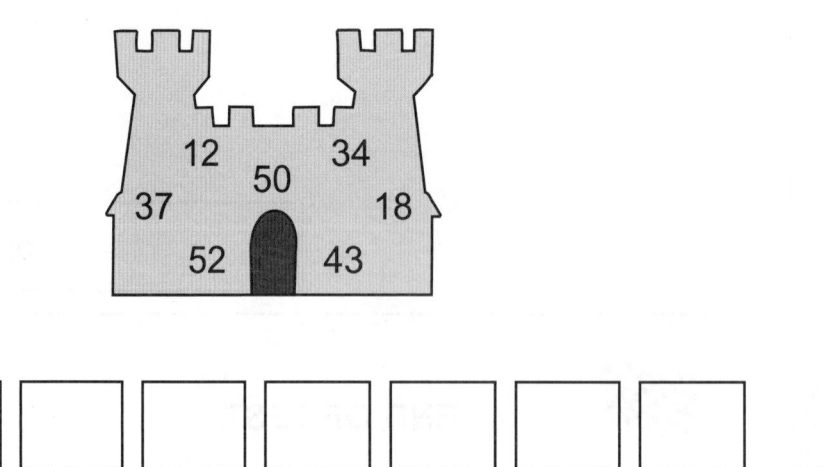

   12, 50, 34, 37, 18, 52, 43

   1 mark

3. Tick **all** of the sentences that are correct.

The morning is the last part of the day. ☐

If today is Monday tomorrow will be Sunday. ☐

The afternoon comes before the evening. ☐

The month before November is October. ☐

1 mark

4. Circle the **two** amounts of money that add up to the total on the piggy bank.

20p   35p

45p   95p   50p

70p   65p

1 mark

You're getting there!

5. Shade $\frac{3}{4}$ of this circle.

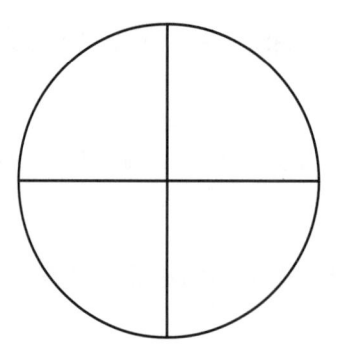

1 mark

6. Put a cross under the clock that shows the wrong time.

half past two   **five past nine**   **quarter to six**

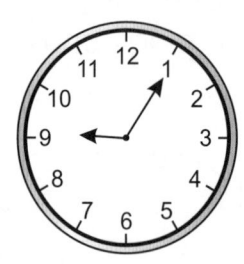

1 mark

7. Sid has **40** blocks.

He shares the blocks equally between **5** friends.

How many blocks does each friend get?

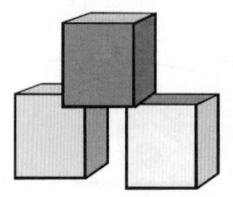

blocks

1 mark

Set B: Test 4

8. Some families are on holiday at a campsite.

   18 families go home.

   There are **23** families left.

   How many families were there to begin with?

   | families |

   1 mark

9. This table shows how many ice creams Dev and his friends ate in the summer holiday.

Child	Number of Ice Creams
Dev	7
Ella	9
Max	5

   How many **more** ice creams did Ella eat than Max?

   | ice creams |

   How many ice creams were eaten **altogether**?

   | ice creams |

   2 marks

   END OF TEST

   | / 10 |

Set B: Arithmetic Test

There are **12 questions**. Give yourself **10 minutes** to answer them.

1. 45 + 4

   1 mark

2. 75 − 7

   1 mark

3. 29 + ☐ = 37

   1 mark

4. 2 × 9

   1 mark

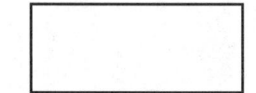

5. 60 + 22

☐ _____
           1 mark

6. 65 + 5 + 5

☐ _____
           1 mark

7. 52 − 15

☐ _____
           1 mark

8. 5 × 10

☐ _____
           1 mark

9. $\frac{1}{2}$ of 16

1 mark

10. 70 ÷ 10

1 mark

11. 81 − ☐ = 38

1 mark

12. $\frac{1}{3}$ of 12

1 mark

END OF TEST

/ 12

Set B: Arithmetic Test

End of Set B: Scoresheet

You've finished a full set of tests — well done!

Put your scores in here
to see how you're doing...

	Score	
Test 1		/10
Test 2		/10
Test 3		/10
Test 4		/10
Arithmetic Test		/12
Total		**/52**

...then look up your total score to see what's next:

0 – 17	You might need some **more practice**. Ask an adult to help, then try the tests again.
18 – 35	**Go back** over the questions you got **wrong**, then try the **next set** of tests.
36 – 52	Well done! Try to beat your score on the **next set** of tests.

But first... bend your brain round this:

Look at these 2D shapes.

Which 3D shape can you make by using these five shapes as faces?

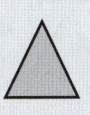

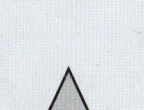

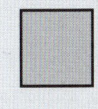

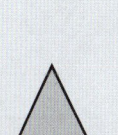

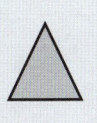

This page may be photocopied

Set C: Test 1

There are **9 questions**. Give yourself **10 minutes** to answer them.

1. Tick the pot that is **more than half full**.

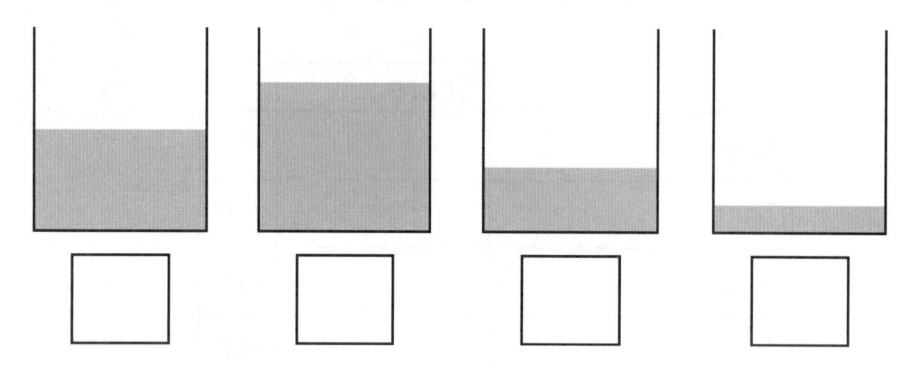

   1 mark

2. Look at this subtraction. $21 - 3$

   Draw an arrow pointing to its answer on the number line.

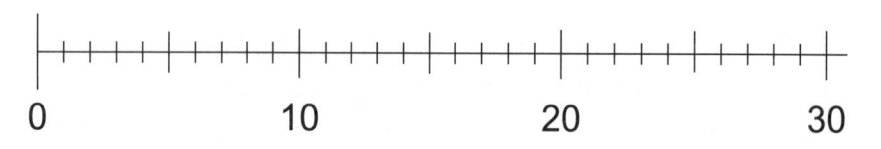

   1 mark

3. Tick the group where $\frac{1}{3}$ of the shapes are **triangles**.

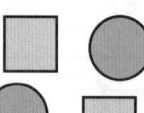

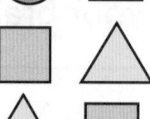

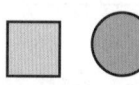

   1 mark

4. Katie eats **12** grapes.

She now has **35** grapes.

How many grapes did she have to begin with?

grapes

1 mark

5. This table shows the lessons Tom has this week.

	Morning	**Afternoon**
Monday	Maths	English
Tuesday	Maths	Art
Wednesday	English	Music
Thursday	Sport	Maths
Friday	English	French

How many **maths** lessons does he have altogether?

maths lessons

1 mark

6. Put a tick inside **all** of the shapes that have a **face** that is a **circle**.

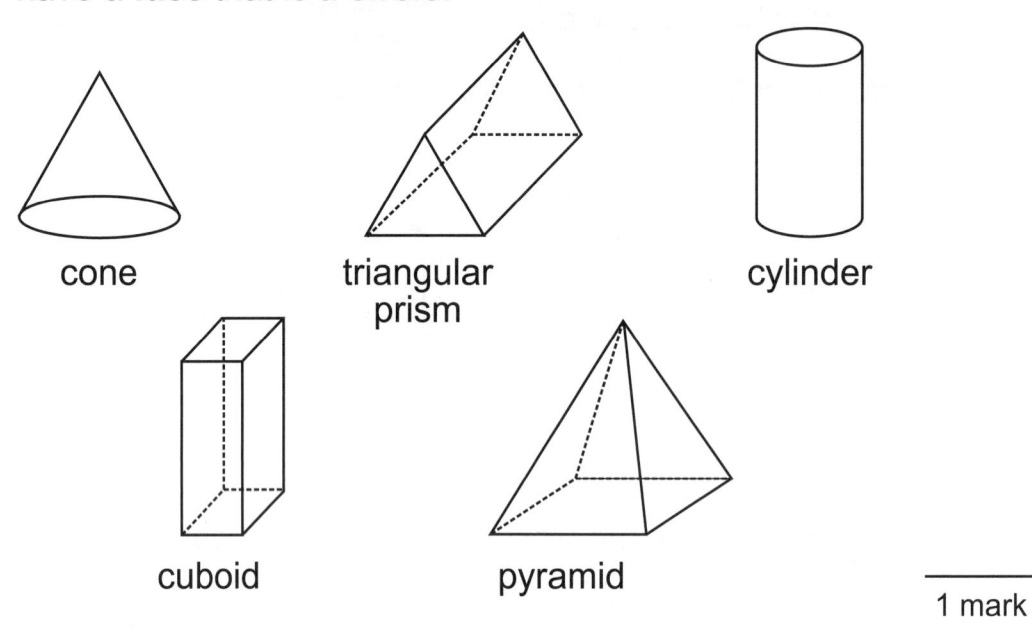

cone

triangular prism

cylinder

cuboid

pyramid

1 mark

7. Naga has **£1**. She buys an orange for **30p**.

Circle the group of coins that she has left.

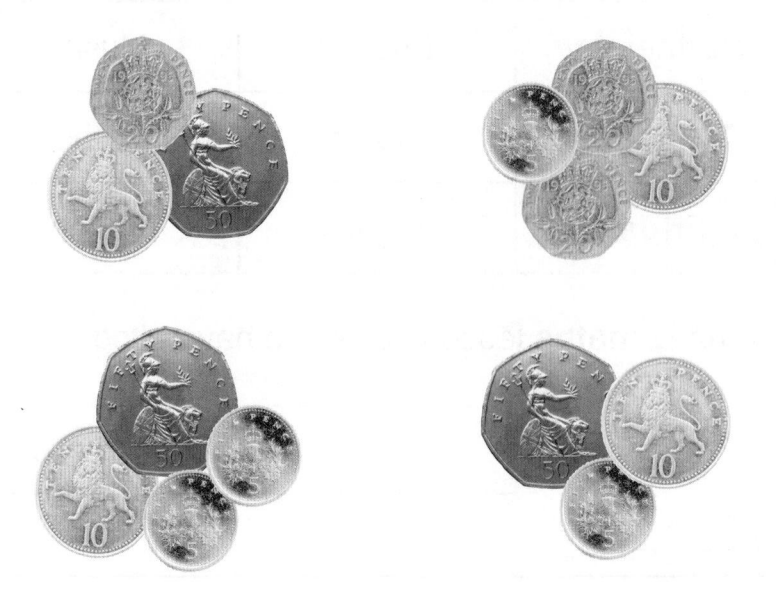

1 mark

Set C: Test 1   44   © CGP — not to be photocopied

8. Write **longer** or **shorter** in the boxes to make each sentence correct.

1 hour is [　　　　　　] than 90 minutes.

1 day is [　　　　　　] than 20 hours.

1 mark

9. There are **25** birds in a garden.

7 more birds land in the garden.

12 birds fly away.

How many birds are in the garden now?

Show your working.

[　　　　　] birds

2 marks

END OF TEST

[/ 10]

Set C: Test 2

There are **9 questions**. Give yourself **10 minutes** to answer them.

1. Draw lines to match each car to the correct flag.

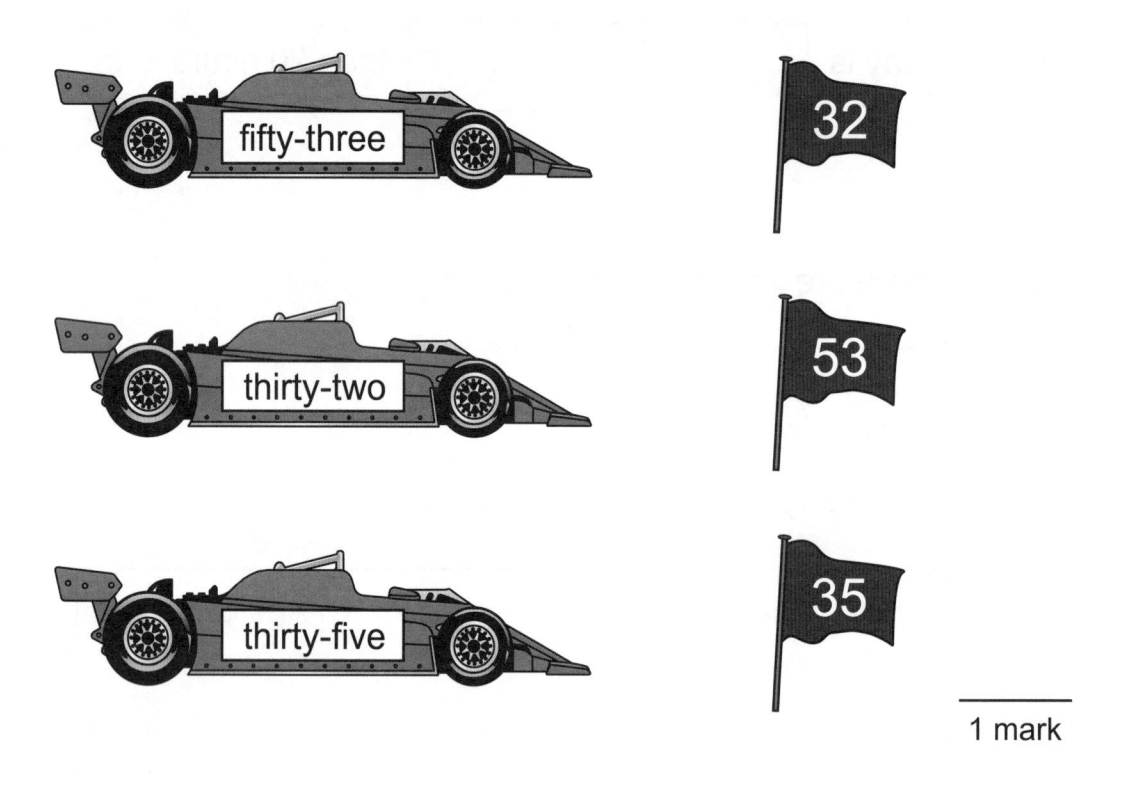

   fifty-three

   thirty-two

   thirty-five

   32

   53

   35

   1 mark

2. Paul has **26** toy dinosaurs.

   Amie has **24** toy dinosaurs.

   How many toy dinosaurs do they have in total?

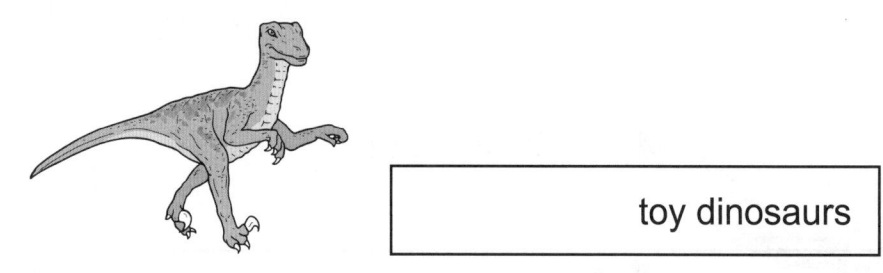

   ☐ toy dinosaurs

   1 mark

Set C: Test 2

3. Circle **all** the hats that have **even** numbers.

10   82   21

39   56   93

1 mark

4. Look at the 3D shapes below.

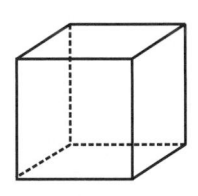

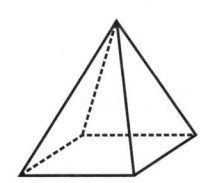

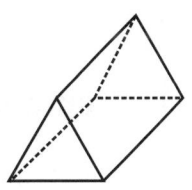

Complete the sentences by filling in the boxes.

A **triangular prism** has ☐ edges.

A ☐ has **8** vertices.

2 marks

5. This is how long it took four friends to find a hidden Easter egg.

Nate	Troy	Gabby	Shona
5 minutes 25 seconds	2 minutes 30 seconds	10 minutes 35 seconds	2 minutes 10 seconds

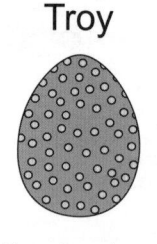

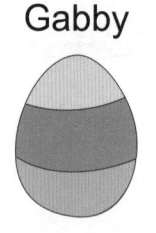

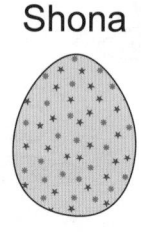

Who found their egg **first**?

1 mark

6. Write the **temperature** in the box.

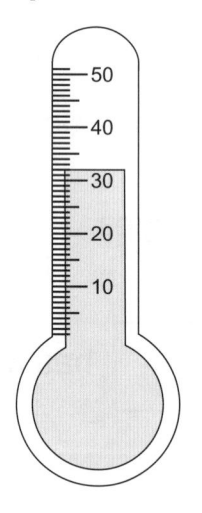

°C

1 mark

7. Write a number in each box to make the number sentences true.

9 – 2 > ☐   11 + 3 < ☐

1 mark

Set C: Test 2   48   © CGP — not to be photocopied

8. There are **12** boats on a lake.

   There are **2** sailors on each one.

   How many sailors are there altogether?

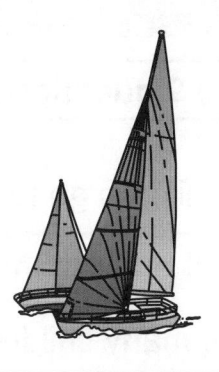

   ☐ sailors

   1 mark

9. This pictogram shows the number of doughnuts Jamie's family ate this summer.

   stands for → 2 doughnuts

   June: 🍩 🍩 🍩 🌗
   July: 🍩 🍩
   August: 🍩 🍩 🍩 🍩 🍩

   How many doughnuts did they eat in **June**?

   ☐ doughnuts

   1 mark

   END OF TEST

   / 10

Set C: Test 3

There are **9 questions**. Give yourself **10 minutes** to answer them.

1. **13** children go to the zoo.

    4 of them visit the **giraffes**. The rest visit the **zebras**.

    How many children visit the **zebras**?

children

    1 mark

2. Draw lines to match each sentence to the correct number.

Number of days in one week		Number of days in April		Number of months in one year

    twelve   seven   thirty

    1 mark

3. Fill in the next three numbers in this sequence.

    3, 6, 9, ☐, ☐, ☐

    1 mark

4. Draw **one line of symmetry** on each shape.

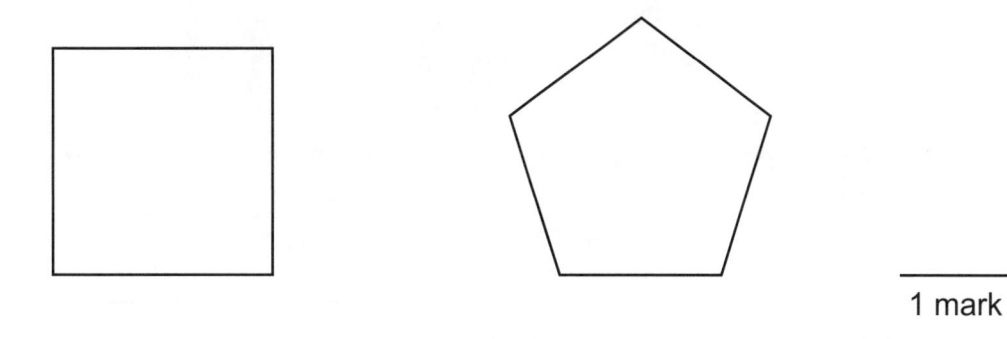

1 mark

5. This block diagram shows the dogs on Matt's street.

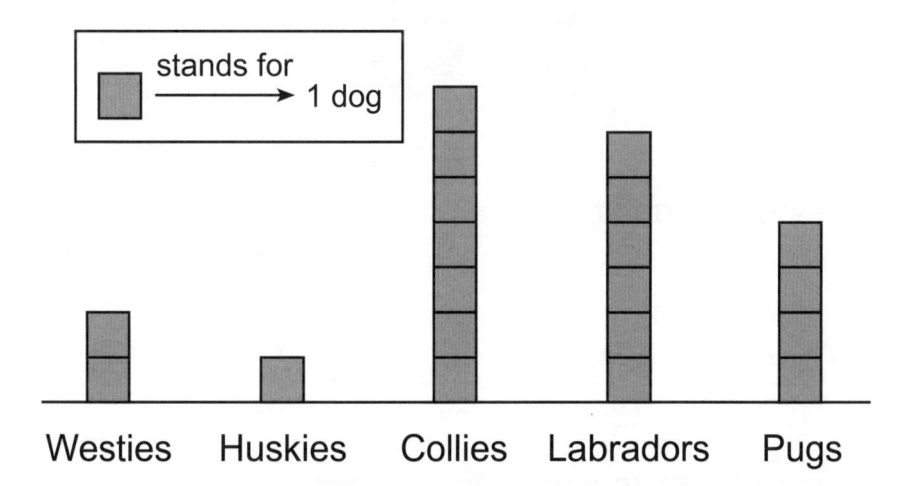

■ stands for → 1 dog

Westies   Huskies   Collies   Labradors   Pugs

How many dogs are there **in total**? ☐ dogs

1 mark

6. Jon has these coins in his pocket.

   What do Jon's coins add up to? [   ] pence

   Jon buys some sweets. He has these coins left over.

   How much did Jon spend? [   ] pence

   2 marks

7. Belle has **10** rabbits and some hutches.

   She puts **2** rabbits in each hutch.

   How many hutches does Belle have?

   [   ] hutches

   1 mark

8. Circle the **two** fractions that are **equal**.

$$\frac{1}{2} \qquad \frac{1}{3} \qquad \frac{3}{4}$$

$$\frac{1}{4} \qquad \frac{2}{4}$$

1 mark

9. A bookcase has **4** shelves.

Each shelf has **5** books on it.

Tick **two** calculations that will show how many books there are altogether.

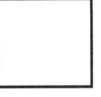

4 + 4 + 4 + 4 ☐   4 × 5 ☐

5 + 5 + 5 + 5 ☐   4 + 5 ☐

1 mark

END OF TEST

/ 10

Set C: Test 4

There are **9 questions**. Give yourself **10 minutes** to answer them.

1. Circle the animal that matches this description.

   It is **in front** of the house.

   It is **below** a window.

   It is to the **right** of the door.

   1 mark

2. Draw lines to match each number to the correct words.

   | 62 | 66 | 16 | 26 |

   - two tens and six ones
   - one ten and six ones
   - six tens and two ones
   - six tens and six ones

   1 mark

3. Cross out the shape that **doesn't** fit the pattern.

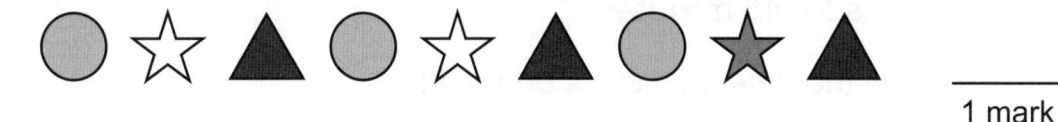

○ ☆ ▲ ○ ☆ ▲ ○ ★ ▲

1 mark

4. Circle **three** numbers that add up to **20**.

8   5

4   9

10   3

1 mark

5. This tally chart shows how many computer games Adam and his friends have.

Name	Tally
Adam	卌 卌 ||
Greg	卌	
Fay	卌 卌	

How many **fewer** games does **Greg** have than **Fay**?

☐ games

1 mark

6. Lou's swimming lesson starts at **10 o'clock**.

   It lasts for **45 minutes**.

   Draw the time it finishes on the clock.

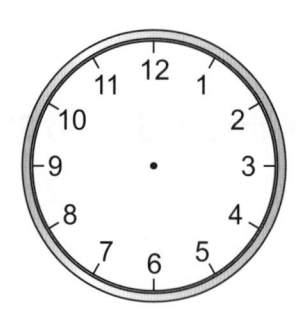

   1 mark

7. In a sports game, Vinny scored **12** points.

   Kali scored **15** points.

   Lena scored **9** points.

   How many points were scored in total?

   Show your working.

   _____ points

   2 marks

Set C: Test 4

8. Look at this boat.

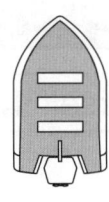

Each picture shows the boat **after** it has made a turn.

Draw lines to match each picture to the correct description.

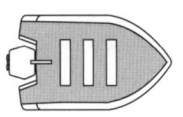

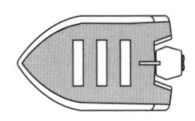

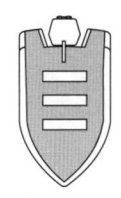

quarter turn clockwise

two quarter turns clockwise

quarter turn anti-clockwise

1 mark

9. Omar has found **8** shells.

He gives $\frac{3}{4}$ of the shells to Rachel.

How many shells does he give to Rachel?

shells

1 mark

END OF TEST

/ 10

Set C: Arithmetic Test

There are **12 questions**. Give yourself **10 minutes** to answer them.

1. 23 − 6

    1 mark

2. 63 + 5

    1 mark

3. 3 × 5

    1 mark

4. 26 + 14

    1 mark

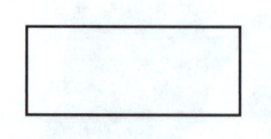

5. 44 − ☐ = 35

1 mark

6. 30 + 20 + 40

☐

1 mark

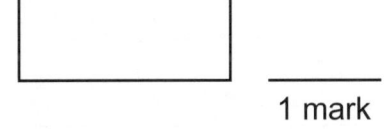

7. 64 − 38

☐

1 mark

8. $\frac{1}{2}$ of 8

☐

1 mark

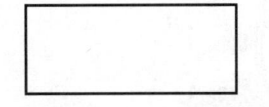

9. 4 × 3

[ ]

1 mark

10. 67 + [ ] = 90

1 mark

11. 18 ÷ 2

[ ]

1 mark

12. $\frac{1}{4}$ of 12

[ ]

1 mark

END OF TEST

[ ] / 12

Set C: Arithmetic Test

End of Set C: Scoresheet

You've finished a full set of tests — well done!

Put your scores in here to see how you're doing...

	Score	
Test 1		/10
Test 2		/10
Test 3		/10
Test 4		/10
Arithmetic Test		/12
Total		**/52**

...then look up your total score in the table below:

0 – 17	You might need some **more practice**. Ask an adult to explain the questions you found tricky.
18 – 35	Go back over the questions you got **wrong** and have **another go**.
36 – 52	You've done really well — great work!

One last thing... bend your brain round this:

Use the weights to balance the scales.

What's the smallest number of weights you can use?

50 g

20 g   10 g   5 g

5 g   10 g   20 g

Answers

Set A

Test 1 — pages 2-5

1. **1 mark for all correct**

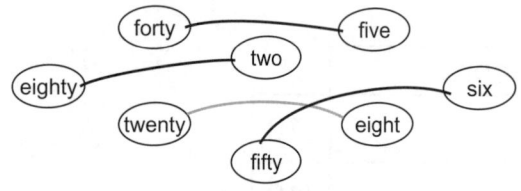

    Topic tested: NUMBERS TO 100

2. **1 mark for all three correct**

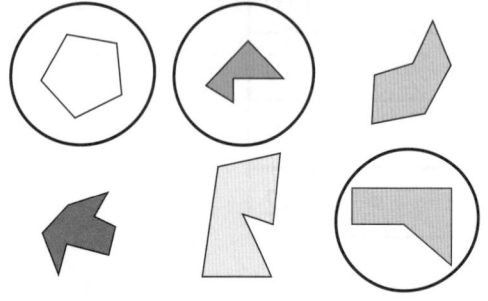

    Topic tested: FLAT (2D) SHAPES

3. **1 mark**

    A tiger weighs 100 **kg**.
    A mouse is 8 **cm** long.
    There is 300 **ml** of juice in my bottle.
    Topic tested: UNITS

4. **1 mark**

    16 pets
    Topic tested: TABLES

5. **1 mark**

    52 > 45
    Topic tested:
    ORDERING AND COMPARING NUMBERS

6. **1 mark**

    2 slices
    Topic tested: FRACTIONS OF AMOUNTS

7. **1 mark**

    Topic tested: MONEY

8. **1 mark**

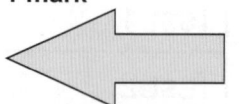

    Topic tested: TURNS

9. **2 marks for correct answer otherwise 1 mark for correct working**

    36 − 17 = 19
    19 − 11 = 8 people
    Topic tested: SUBTRACTING

Test 2 — pages 6-9

1. **1 mark for both correct**

    57
    61
    Topic tested: ODD AND EVEN NUMBERS

2. **1 mark**

    14 green pencils
    Topic tested: SUBTRACTING

3. **1 mark**

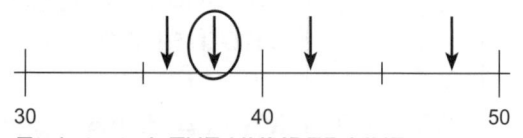

    Topic tested: THE NUMBER LINE

4. **1 mark**

    250 grams
    Topic tested: MEASURING

5. **1 mark**

    Jack
    Topic tested: TIME

6. **1 mark**

    12 books
    Topic tested: FRACTIONS OF AMOUNTS

Answers

Answers

7. 1 mark for each correct answer

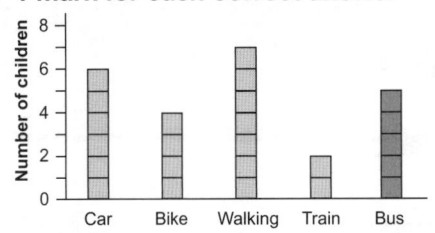

5 children
Topic tested: BLOCK DIAGRAMS

8. 1 mark

45 people
Topic tested: MULTIPLYING

9. 1 mark for 3 correct coins

Accept any answer where both 20p coins and one 50p coin are circled, e.g.

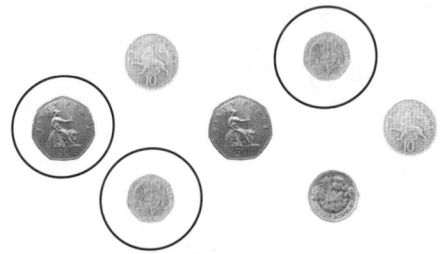

Topic tested: SUMS WITH MONEY

Test 3 — pages 10-13

1. 1 mark for all four correct

42, 47, 63, 55
Topic tested: PLACE VALUE

2. 1 mark

May
Topic tested: DATES

3. 1 mark

77 pies
Topic tested: ADDING

4. 1 mark

Topic tested: PICTOGRAMS

5. 1 mark

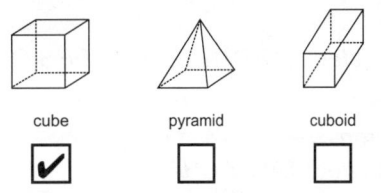

cube — ✓   pyramid   cuboid
Topic tested: SOLID (3D) SHAPES

6. 1 mark for all three correct

before
after
first
Topic tested: COMPARING TIME

7. 1 mark

8 children
Topic tested: DIVIDING

8. 1 mark for each correct fraction

$\frac{1}{3}$

$\frac{1}{2}$ (accept $\frac{2}{4}$)

Topic tested: FRACTIONS

9. 1 mark for both correct

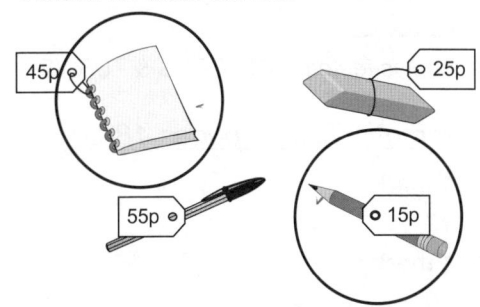

45p, 25p, 55p, 15p

Topic tested: SUMS WITH MONEY

Test 4 — pages 14-17

1. 1 mark

39 balloons
Topic tested: ADDING

2. 1 mark

366
Topic tested: DATES

3. 1 mark

1 (one)
Topic tested: 3D (SOLID) SHAPES

Answers

4. **1 mark for both correct**
   82, 52
   Topic tested: COUNTING IN STEPS OF 10

5. **1 mark**
   5 children
   Topic tested: TALLY CHARTS

6. **1 mark for all correct**
   D, B, A, C
   Topic tested: COMPARING MEASUREMENTS

7. **2 marks for correct answer otherwise 1 mark for correct working**
   9 + 7 = 16
   16 − 3 = 13 presents
   Topics tested: ADDING & SUBTRACTING

8. **1 mark for both correct**
   44
   12
   Topics tested: ADDING

9. **1 mark** 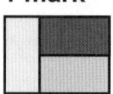
   Topics tested: PATTERNS & TURNS

Arithmetic Test — pages 18-20

1. **1 mark**
   12
2. **1 mark**
   30
3. **1 mark**
   50
4. **1 mark**
   14
5. **1 mark**
   71
6. **1 mark**
   36
7. **1 mark**
   22
8. **1 mark**
   60
9. **1 mark**
   11
10. **1 mark**
    57
11. **1 mark**
    9
12. **1 mark**
    30

Scoresheet Question — page 21

There are 4 different ways:
£1 coin
50p + 50p
50p + 20p + 20p + 5p + 5p (twice, with the two different 50p coins).

Set B

Test 1 — pages 22-25

1. **1 mark for both correct**
   seventy-three
   twenty-five
   Topic tested: TENS AND ONES

2. **1 mark for all four correct** 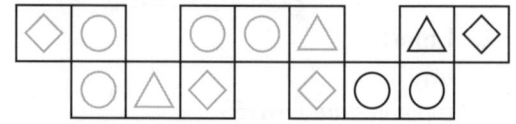
   Topic tested: ORDERING AND PATTERNS

3. **1 mark for both correct**
   There are 24 hours in a day.
   There are 12 months in a year.
   Topics tested: DAYS, DATES & TIME

Answers

4. 1 mark for 3 correct coins

Accept any answer where the 10p, 20p and any one 5p are circled, e.g.

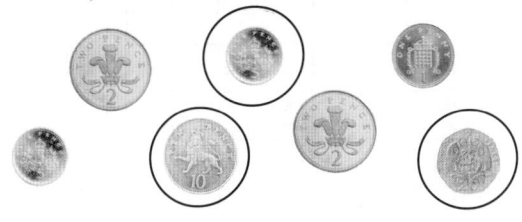

Topic tested: MONEY

5. 1 mark

weight of spinner > weight of car
Topic tested:
COMPARING MEASUREMENTS

6. 1 mark

2 birds
Topic tested: BLOCK DIAGRAMS

7. 1 mark

20 sheep
Topic tested: HALVES

8. 1 mark for each correct answer

65 (accept 64 or 66)
82 (accept 81 or 83)
Topic tested: THE NUMBER LINE

9. 1 mark

19 blackberries
Topic tested: SUBTRACTING

Test 2 — pages 26-29

1. 1 mark for all four correct

backwards up forwards down

← ↑ → ↓

Topic tested: DIRECTION

2. 1 mark

23 animals
Topic tested: SUBTRACTING

3. 1 mark for both correct

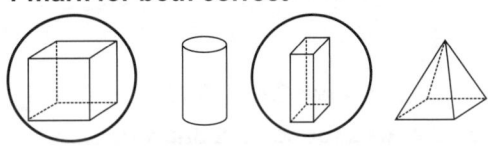

Topic tested: SOLID (3D) SHAPES

4. 1 mark for both correct

slower
before
Topic tested: COMPARING TIME

5. 1 mark for all three correct

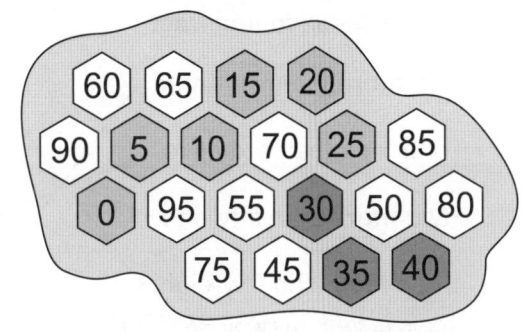

Topic tested: COUNTING IN STEPS OF 5

6. 1 mark for all correct

Meal	Tally	Total
Pizza	|||| ||||		11
Roast Dinner	|||| |||	8
Curry	||||	4

Topic tested: TALLY CHARTS

7. 1 mark

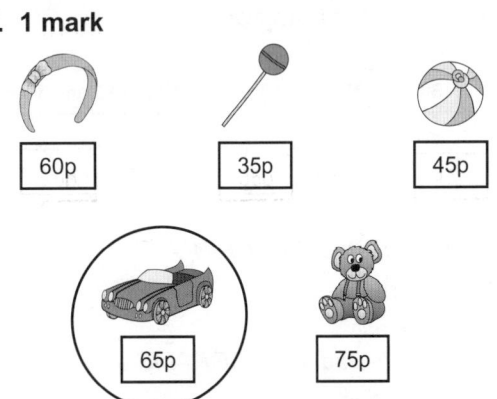

60p   35p   45p

65p   75p

Topic tested: SUMS WITH MONEY

Answers

8. **1 mark for both correct**

   37 + 10
   47 − 37
   Topic tested: CHECKING

9. **2 marks for correct answer otherwise 1 mark for correct working**

   27 + 8 = 35
   35 + 9 = 44 children
   Topic tested: ADDING

Test 3 — pages 30-33

1. **1 mark for all four correct**

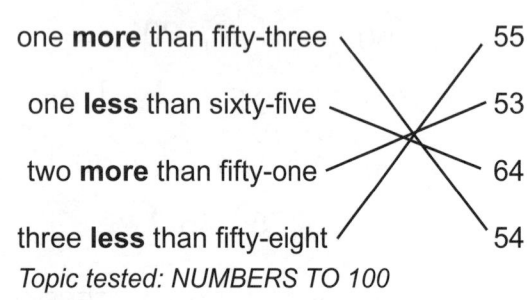

   one **more** than fifty-three — 55
   one **less** than sixty-five — 53
   two **more** than fifty-one — 64
   three **less** than fifty-eight — 54
   Topic tested: NUMBERS TO 100

2. **1 mark**

   Triangle
   Topic tested: SOLID (3D) SHAPES

3. **1 mark**

   60 minutes
   Topics Tested: TIME

4. **1 mark**

   35 ml
   Topic tested: MEASURING

5. **1 mark for both correct**

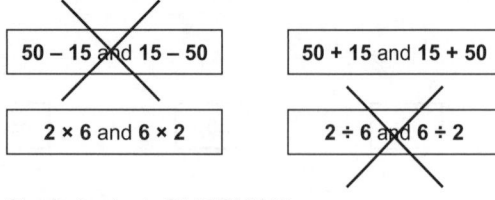

   | 50 − 15 and 15 − 50 | (crossed out) | 50 + 15 and 15 + 50 |
   | 2 × 6 and 6 × 2 | 2 ÷ 6 and 6 ÷ 2 (crossed out) |

   Topic tested: CHECKING

6. **1 mark**

   3 leaves
   Topic tested: PICTOGRAMS

7. **1 mark**

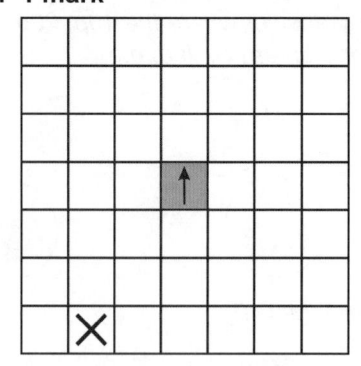

   Topics tested: DIRECTION & TURNS

8. **1 mark**

   30 children
   Topic tested: MULTIPLYING

9. **2 marks for correct answer otherwise 1 mark for correct working**

   83 − 30 = 53
   53 + 7 = 60 coins
   Topics tested: ADDING & SUBTRACTING

Test 4 — pages 34-37

1. **1 mark for all three correct objects crossed out**

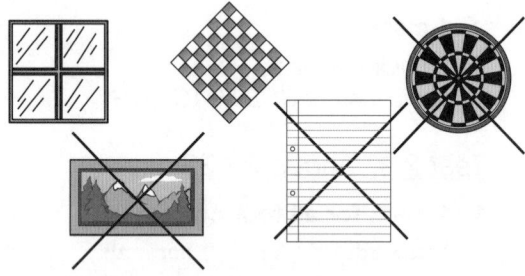

   Topic tested: FLAT (2D) SHAPES

2. **1 mark for correct order**

   12, 18, 34, 37, 43, 50, 52
   Topic tested: ORDERING

3. **1 mark for both correct**

   The afternoon comes before the evening.
   The month before November is October.
   Topic tested: DAYS & DATES

Answers

4. **1 mark for both correct**
   45p
   50p
   Topic tested: MONEY

5. **1 mark for any answer where 3 sectors are shaded**
   E.g.

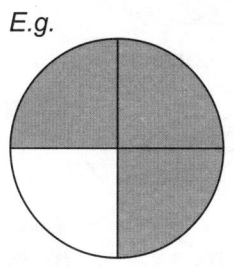

   Topic tested: QUARTERS

6. **1 mark**
   half past two   five past nine   quarter to six

   ✗

   Topic tested: TIME

7. **1 mark**
   8 blocks
   Topic tested: DIVIDING

8. **1 mark**
   41 families
   Topic tested: ADDING

9. **1 mark for each correct answer**
   4 ice creams
   21 ice creams
   Topic tested: TABLES

Arithmetic Test — pages 38-40

1. **1 mark**
   49
2. **1 mark**
   68
3. **1 mark**
   8

4. **1 mark**
   18
5. **1 mark**
   82
6. **1 mark**
   75
7. **1 mark**
   37
8. **1 mark**
   50
9. **1 mark**
   8
10. **1 mark**
    7
11. **1 mark**
    43
12. **1 mark**
    4

Scoresheet Question — page 41

A square-based pyramid

Set C

Test 1 — pages 42-45

1. **1 mark**

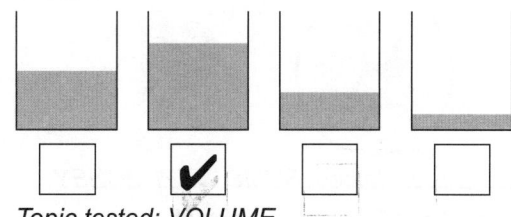

   Topic tested: VOLUME

2. **1 mark**

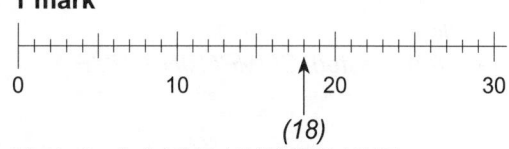

   (18)

   Topic tested: THE NUMBER LINE

Answers

3. 1 mark

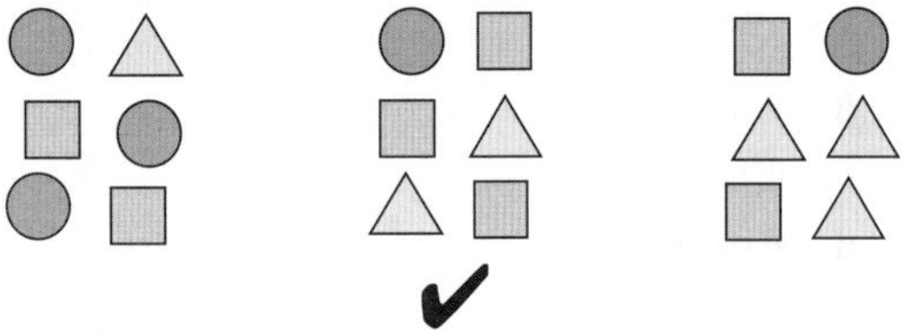

Topic tested: FRACTIONS OF AMOUNTS

4. 1 mark

47 grapes
Topic tested: ADDING

5. 1 mark

3 maths lessons
Topic tested: TABLES

6. 1 mark for both correct objects ticked

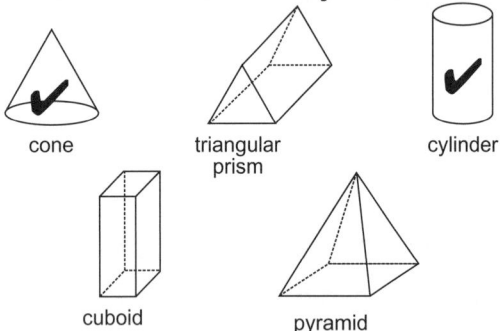

cone ✓
triangular prism
cylinder ✓
cuboid
pyramid

Topic tested: SOLID (3D) SHAPES

7. 1 mark

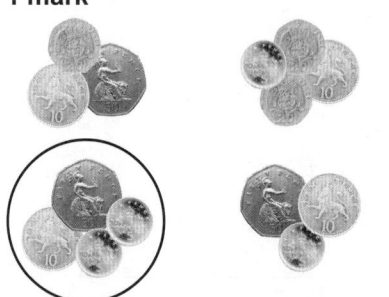

Topic tested: SUMS WITH MONEY

8. 1 mark for both correct

shorter
longer
Topic tested: COMPARING TIME

9. 2 marks for correct answer otherwise 1 mark for correct working

25 + 7 = 32
32 − 12 = 20 birds
Topics tested: ADDING & SUBTRACTING

Test 2 — pages 46-49

1. 1 mark for all three correct

fifty-three — 53
thirty-two — 32
thirty-five — 35

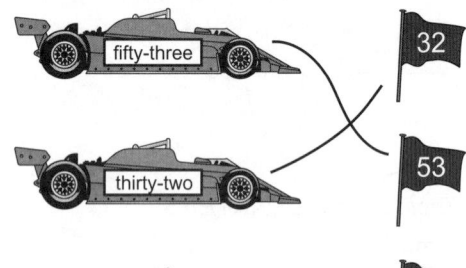

Topic tested: NUMBERS TO 100

2. 1 mark

50 toy dinosaurs
Topic tested: ADDING

3. 1 mark for all three correct hats circled

10, 82, 56

Topic tested: ODD AND EVEN NUMBERS

4. 1 mark for each correct answer

nine (9)
cube (accept cuboid)
Topic tested: SOLID (3D) SHAPES

5. 1 mark

Shona
Topic tested: COMPARING TIME

6. 1 mark

32 °C
Topic tested: MEASURING

Answers

Answers

7. 1 mark for both correct

Number sentence 1: Accept any number less than or equal to 6, e.g. 9 – 2 > 5.
Number sentence 2: Accept any number greater than or equal to 15, e.g. 11 + 3 < 16.

Topic tested:
ORDERING AND COMPARING NUMBERS

8. 1 mark

24 sailors
Topic tested: MULTIPLYING

9. 1 mark

7 doughnuts
Topic tested: PICTOGRAMS

Test 3 — pages 50-53

1. 1 mark

9 children
Topic tested: SUBTRACTING

2. 1 mark for all three correct

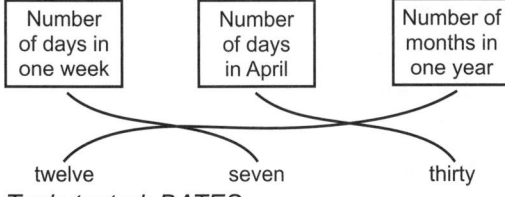

Number of days in one week — seven
Number of days in April — thirty
Number of months in one year — twelve

Topic tested: DATES

3. 1 mark for all three numbers correct

12, 15, 18
Topic tested:
COUNTING IN STEPS OF THREE

4. 1 mark for a correct line of symmetry drawn on each shape

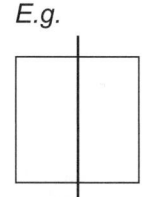

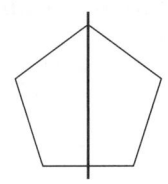

E.g.

Accept any other correct lines of symmetry.
Topic tested: FLAT (2D) SHAPES

5. 1 mark

20 dogs
Topic tested: BLOCK DIAGRAMS

6. 1 mark for each correct answer

89 pence
65 pence
Topics tested: MONEY

7. 1 mark

5 hutches
Topic tested: DIVIDING

8. 1 mark for both correct

$\frac{1}{2}, \frac{2}{4}$

Topic tested: EQUIVALENT FRACTIONS

9. 1 mark for both correct calculations ticked

5 + 5 + 5 + 5
4 × 5
Topic tested: MULTIPLYING

Test 4 — pages 54-57

1. 1 mark

Topic tested: POSITION

2. 1 mark for all four correctly matched

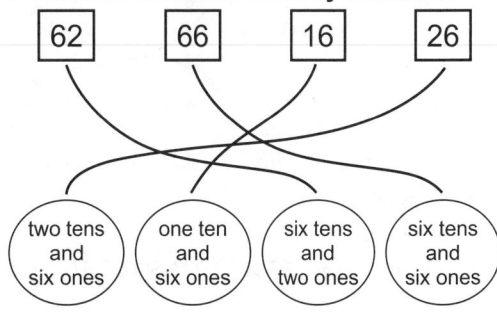

62 — six tens and two ones
66 — six tens and six ones
16 — one ten and six ones
26 — two tens and six ones

Topic tested: NUMBERS TO 100

Answers

3. 1 mark

○ ☆ ▲ ○ ☆ ▲ ○ ✷ ▲

Topic tested: ORDERING AND PATTERNS

4. 1 mark for all three correct numbers

8, 3, 9
Topic tested: ADDING

5. 1 mark

5 games
Topic tested: TALLY CHARTS

6. 1 mark

Accept any answer where the minute hand is correctly positioned and the hour hand is between 10 and 11.
Topic tested: TIME

7. 2 marks for correct answer otherwise 1 mark for correct working

12 + 15 = 27
27 + 9 = 36 points
Topic tested: ADDING

8. 1 mark for all three correctly matched

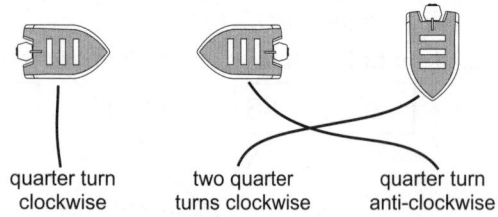

quarter turn clockwise   two quarter turns clockwise   quarter turn anti-clockwise
Topic tested: DIRECTION AND TURNS

9. 1 mark

6 shells
Topic tested: FRACTIONS OF AMOUNTS

Arithmetic Test — pages 58-60

1. 1 mark
17

2. 1 mark
68

3. 1 mark
15

4. 1 mark
40

5. 1 mark
9

6. 1 mark
90

7. 1 mark
26

8. 1 mark
4

9. 1 mark
12

10. 1 mark
23

11. 1 mark
9

12. 1 mark
3

Scoresheet Question — page 61

Smallest number of weights is 3 (20 g + 20 g + 10 g).
Other possible combinations are:
20 g + 20 g + 5 g + 5 g
20 g + 10 g + 10 g + 5 g + 5 g